ELT Development Series

SERIES EDITOR Thomas S. C. Farrell

Second Language Acquisition Applied to English Language Teaching

Michael Lessard-Clouston

 tesolpress

www.tesol.org/bookstore

TESOL International Association
1925 Ballenger Avenue
Alexandria, Virginia, 22314 USA
www.tesol.org

Director of Publishing and Product Development: Myrna Jacobs
Copy Editor: Sarah Duffy
Cover: Citrine Sky Design
Interior Design & Layout: Capitol Communications, LLC
Printing: Gasch Printing, LLC

ISBN 978-1-942799-94-8
Library of Congress Control Number 2017954014

Table of Contents

Acknowledgements

An early, preliminary version of aspects of Chapter 8 appeared in the online proceedings for the 2007 CATESOL State Conference. I would also like to express my sincere gratitude to my professors at OISE/UT for their wonderful teaching about SLA; all my SLA students, who help refine my understanding of L2 learning and teaching; my sons Joel and Caleb, for enabling me to truly see language learning in practice; and Tom Farrell, series editor extraordinaire, for his many insightful comments and suggestions.

Series Editor's Preface

The English Language Teacher Development (ELTD) series consists of a set of short resource books for ESL/EFL teachers that are written in a jargon-free and accessible manner for all types of teachers of English (native, nonnative, experienced, and novice teachers). The ELTD series is designed to offer teachers a theory-to-practice approach to second language teaching, and each book offers a wide variety of practical teaching approaches and methods for the topic at hand. Each book also offers time for reflections for each teacher to interact with the materials presented in the book. The books can be used in preservice settings or in in-service courses and can also be used by individuals looking for ways to refresh their practice.

Michael Lessard-Clouston's book, *Second Language Acquisition Applied to Language Teaching*, explores the relevance of second language acquisition (SLA) theory to English language teaching. Lessard-Clouston explains in detail what SLA is and how it can be used by English language teachers in their classroom lessons. After outlining and discussing three essentials of SLA (input, output, and interaction), the book discusses how age and anxiety impact language learning as well as issues related to error correction and developing materials that reflect SLA principles. The book ends with a discussion of what SLA offers English language teachers.

Second Language Acquisition Applied to Language Teaching is another valuable addition to the literature in our profession and to the ELTD series.

I am very grateful to the authors who contributed to the ELTD series for sharing their knowledge and expertise with other TESOL professionals. It is truly an honor for me to work with each of these authors as they selflessly give up their valuable time for the advancement of TESOL.

Thomas S. C. Farrell

CHAPTER 1

Second Language Acquisition Provides an Understanding of Teachers and Students

This book is about second language acquisition and its applications to English language teaching. Yet we first need to establish what we mean by *second language acquisition* (SLA) in order to consider potential ways to apply it in teaching students of English as a second or foreign language (ESL/EFL). This introductory chapter does this and provides an overview of English language teachers and their students as (second) language users.

What Is SLA?

Throughout this book I want to engage you, my reader, directly in thinking about SLA and English language teaching (ELT). Please therefore stop and reflect by answering the question below as we start. Then write down your definition(s) of, or thoughts on, SLA.

REFLECTIVE QUESTION

- What is your definition of second language acquisition?

Learning/being educated in a language which one is working to become proficient in.

In essence, SLA deals with people learning a second or foreign language (L2/FL) but includes all languages one has acquired subsequent to learning their first language (L1), or mother tongue.

Research shows that the line is sometimes blurred between one's first and other languages, especially when children grow up hearing and using two languages from birth, as is increasingly common in urban contexts. This is now often referred to as bilingual first language acquisition (De Houwer, 2009). Whether or not one grows up bilingual (using two languages), second language acquisition may be defined as older children and adults learning subsequent languages later in life, in addition to their first language(s).

Teachers Can Use L2/FL Learning Experiences

I, for example, grew up in Toronto using English and later studied French in high school and Spanish at university. My French and Spanish acquisition therefore reflects SLA, and later I learned some Chinese and Japanese as I taught for extended periods in China and Japan. Although I studied French and Spanish in L2 classrooms, I didn't learn Chinese and Japanese that way; instead I acquired something of those languages naturally for communication and survival in China and Japan. All four languages are included in my SLA, although the contexts were very different. Already, we begin to glimpse the complexity of SLA, which may include natural language learning beyond one's mother tongue (like my experiences with Chinese and Japanese) and instructional contexts in L2/FL classrooms (such as my French and Spanish learning). French is my strongest L2, yet I retain receptive knowledge of the other languages and can use greetings or other helpful phrases in Chinese, Japanese, and Spanish when useful.

This is a good place to ask you to consider your language learning in a reflective break.

REFLECTIVE QUESTIONS

- What is your mother tongue, or your L1? What other languages have you learned? In what contexts? What observations might you make about them?

One of the joys of working with ESL/EFL students is that teachers who have learned additional languages, including teachers who are nonnative English speakers, can draw on and frankly share about their natural or classroom L2/FL learning as they teach, encourage, and support their students in the challenging task of English language learning.

All teachers with SLA experience should use that knowledge to help their students learn. In my case, I have been able to connect and share with French- and Spanish-speaking ESL students that I have taught in Canada, noting relevant similarities and differences. French–English similarities include many cognates, words that have similar origins, such as *government* and *gouvernement*, as our English word actually comes from Old French. As for differences, false friends are words that seem similar but actually have very different usage or meanings, such as *embarrassed* in English and *embarazada* in Spanish, which means pregnant. These are issues we can discuss with our ESL/EFL students when we draw on our knowledge of other languages, whether it be grammar, vocabulary, or cultural issues and pragmatic expectations.

REFLECTIVE QUESTIONS

● What connections between languages are you aware of that you can share with students? How might you incorporate those in your English teaching?

Some specialists (e.g., Gass, Behney, & Plonksy, 2013) do not distinguish between formal or classroom SLA and other learning contexts, such as my experiences in China and Japan. Yet other writers (e.g., Lightbown & Spada, 2013) recognize that there can be important differences depending on the specific L2/FL learning situation. I agree with this latter group.

Understanding Our Students as English Language Learners

Having briefly considered how teachers can draw on their language learning experiences, we should now similarly think about students and develop a correct perspective on them as English language learners (ELLs). Cook (2016) offers a helpful SLA perspective applying L2 user concepts to instruction, noting that the focus in language teaching should be on ESL/EFL learners, not some ideal native English speakers. In essence, Cook realistically defines ESL/EFL students as L2 users who are gaining various levels of *multi-competence*, "the overall system of a mind or a community that uses more than one language" (p. 14).

This multi-competence is different from monolingual native English speakers' experience and knowledge; as students learning English, "L2 users think in different ways to monolinguals" (Cook, 2016, p. 177). In ESL/EFL we are not teaching native English speakers, but instead English language learners. Accordingly, proficient ESL/EFL users should be prominent in our examples, textbooks, and materials, not just native English speakers that they might interact with. Also, ELLs should experience the richness of English use, and we should therefore not hesitate to use codeswitching (using two languages in one sentence when the people know both languages) as appropriate in class, and we must recognize the value of students' native languages for language learning, just as we have teachers' language experience and knowledge for language teaching (for more on codeswitching, see Farrell, 2017). These insights are especially useful when teachers know their students' L1 and are thus able to incorporate it into their teaching when that is helpful (for more on L2 user perspectives on L2 learning and teaching, see Cook & Li, 2016).

REFLECTIVE QUESTIONS

- What is your experience with codeswitching in English language teaching? Are there specific ways that you might occasionally incorporate it in class?

Viewing students as English language learners, rather than as people who are not native English speakers, has implications for ESL/EFL teaching. Major implications include allowing codeswitching and students' L1 in class when useful for their ESL/EFL learning. Cook (2016) notes that codeswitching is a demanding skill that requires knowledge of the two languages, and it is especially relevant for highlighting a concept (including what someone has said), discussing certain topics, and emphasizing particular social roles (p. 189). This is something that proficient L2 users of English do naturally when they are speaking to others who know the two languages. In English class, therefore, teachers and students alike may incorporate codeswitching when it is helpful.

Similarly, Cook (2016) suggests that although the emphasis in most teaching approaches is on English language input, when teachers know their students' L1 it can be efficient and helpful to use it occasionally in class in order to explain grammar or vocabulary to students, for classroom management or instructions for tasks, and when clarifying things in pair or group activities. This perspective is supported by Hall and Cook's (2014) study on what they call students' "own-language use," which notes that while L1 use in ELT may be more suitable with lower level students, it is also used frequently by teachers to explain meaning, grammar, and vocabulary, and in conjunction with bilingual dictionaries in class. Hall and Cook's findings also highlight the gap concerning the role and use of L1 in ESL/EFL "between mainstream ELT literature and teachers' practices *on the ground*" (p. 39, original emphasis). With these insights, Cook's view is that teachers should first connect with students' goals as much as possible in their teaching in order to support students' English language learning.

REFLECTIVE QUESTIONS

- How do (or might) you use your students' L1 in teaching English? In what specific ways and for what purposes could that prove useful?

- How can you ensure appropriate English language input while also maintaining learner-centredness in your classes?

Conclusion

SLA is the field in applied linguistics that deals with learning any language apart from one's native language, including all additional language learning. Both teachers and learners bring different types of language experience and knowledge to teaching and learning English, and SLA helps us have a correct understanding of ourselves as ESL/EFL teachers and of our students as English language learners and L2 users, as this short book aims to show.

Krashen's Principles of SLA

One early and influential figure in second language acquisition is Stephen Krashen, who posited five principles that still shape topics in the current SLA literature. Outlining these briefly will help us learn about some important topics in SLA for English language teachers.

Acquisition or Learning in the Natural Order

Krashen's (2003) first principle is the *acquisition-learning hypothesis*, which distinguishes specifically between subconscious and conscious learning. Thus, in Krashen's view, *acquisition* refers to incidental, implicit, subconscious, and meaning-focused learning, whereas *learning* is said to only be conscious and formally taught knowledge about language, and there is no interface between what one learns and what one acquires. My limited Chinese and Japanese were acquired, for example, because I didn't study those languages in formal classes, but gained what I did through natural life experience. In contrast, my initial French and most of my Spanish were learned, according to Krashen, because that took place in second or foreign language classrooms where I learned about French and Spanish.

For Krashen, acquisition is how children naturally pick up their first language, in contrast to more traditional, grammar-based classroom language learning.

Like other authors (e.g., Cook, 2016), in this book I do not make a distinction between L2/FL acquisition and learning. Instead, I choose to use those two terms interchangeably. In brief, whether one's L2/FL learning takes place through real-life experience or in a classroom, it may be conscious and/or meaning-based, and for most pedagogical purposes I do not find that distinction to be particularly useful. And most native English speakers also learn their first language in schools, too, through what we often call *English language arts*.

Krashen's (2003) second principle is the *natural order hypothesis*, in which he argues that the learning order for rules of languages, and English in particular, is predictable, can't change, and isn't teachable (p. 2). Native English speakers, for example, acquire the progressive *–ing* pretty early, while the third person singular *–s* on verbs is acquired later. In adult ESL/EFL learning the same is true, though some ESL/EFL students who actually speak very well still struggle with using the third person singular *–s*. This doesn't mean everyone learns all structures in the same order but that there is what Krashen refers to as "an 'average' order of acquisition" (p. 2). Further points here are that (a) while predictable, the so-called natural order is not always obvious, so what may seem simple or complex to educators and linguists does not always translate into clear rules for curriculum developers; (b) this natural order can't be changed, even with repeated explicit drills or clear explanations in the classroom; and (c) the natural order isn't necessarily the teaching order in most ESL/EFL classes, curricula, and textbooks. This principle suggests that grammar points should not be introduced before students are ready to acquire them.

REFLECTIVE QUESTIONS

- What are your thoughts on the acquisition versus learning distinction?

- What specific English grammar points do you think should be taught earlier or later?

The Monitor, Input, and Affective Filter

The third principle from Krashen (2003) is the *Monitor hypothesis*, which states that language "is normally produced using our acquired linguistic competence" and that conscious learning has one main function, to Monitor or edit (p. 2). When a student wants to say something in the target language, a sentence will appear in their mind, and before actually producing it they can use their consciously learned knowledge to correct any error and improve accuracy. They can alternatively use the conscious Monitor to correct sentences after they have produced them.

Yet to use the Monitor successfully, Krashen (2003, p. 3) argues that a student must (a) know the rule, (b) be thinking about the form and correctness, and (c) have time to process this while speaking. In reality, though, many language rules are complicated, it's hard to focus on the correct form *and* meaning at the same time that one is speaking, and most normal conversations do not provide sufficient time for the use of the Monitor. Krashen indicates the "Monitor is weak, but it is not useless," and all three conditions are perhaps most often met on grammar tests. As a result, Krashen's advice is for students to "use the conscious Monitor when it does not interfere with communication, when we have time, as in the editing phase of writing" (p 3).

Krashen's (2003) fourth principle is the *input hypothesis*, which claims that we acquire languages through input when we understand messages. This principle argues that understanding messages is the only way we acquire language, but a great deal of input alone isn't enough; the input must be understood (thus Krashen later referred to this as the *comprehension hypothesis*). Yet Krashen adds two stipulations: (1) Talking isn't really practising, and thus it does not result in language acquisition, and (2) when we offer students enough comprehensible input containing accurate grammar and vocabulary, $i + 1$ (the input slightly above the acquirer's current level of knowledge) will be present, with "plenty of chances for the student to get comprehensible input containing $i + 1$" (p. 5). For individual variation, Krashen argues that using comprehensible input is the best way to help different students acquire language.

Krashen's (2003) final principle is the *affective filter hypothesis*, which states that negative variables block input from reaching the language acquisition device—that "part of the brain responsible for language acquisition" (p. 6). The affective filter keeps out any input when the acquirer is uncomfortable, is nervous, struggles with anxiety or has self-esteem issues, or cannot see themselves as someone who can speak the target language. As a result, Krashen declares that the "presence of the affective filter explains how two students can receive the same (comprehensible) input, yet one makes progress while the other does not" (p. 6). In essence, a high affective filter blocks one student from learning, but a low one does not.

REFLECTIVE QUESTIONS

- How do you encourage students to correct their English language use?

- When and how do your students have access to comprehensible input?

- Do your students struggle with any affective issues in learning English?

Conclusion

As this overview of Krashen's (2003) SLA principles hopefully indicates, many topics are relevant to current English language teaching, including learning processes, what to teach and when, the importance of accuracy and correction, what input is and how to maximize it for students, and how to create an effective learning environment in ESL/EFL classes. This short book helps teachers develop a deeper understanding of SLA by discussing more recent research. (To read more on Krashen's work, consult http://www.sdkrashen.com/.)

REFLECTIVE QUESTIONS

- Which of Krashen's five hypotheses seem most plausible to you? Do any seem problematic? Which are most relevant to your English teaching?

CHAPTER 3

SLA Essential I: Input

The next three chapters introduce essential components of students' ESL/
EFL learning: input, output, and interaction. They also note approaches
to these that can inform and impact one's classroom teaching. We begin
with input.

Input

No matter the theoretical position one takes toward second language
acquisition, everyone agrees that input is an essential condition for second
language learning. Without input, no one can learn a language. Input is
the model language that learners are exposed to, including all the English
that students encounter through listening and reading. In English language
teaching classrooms, input exists in oral and written form, through examples
on the board or on PowerPoint slides, in the materials used (textbooks,
multimedia, readings, etc.), in teacher talk, and in speech or writing from
other learners. In classes, English input may be simplified, as is often the
case in teachers' speech, textbooks, and graded readers, for example. In ESL
contexts, learners also likely have contact with unsimplified input outside
of class as they interact with native and nonnative English speakers, but
virtually all learners today may also be exposed to English input through

entertainment (in films, music, radio, television), social media, and the Internet (e-mail, websites, YouTube, etc.).

Ellis (2015) distinguishes between non-interactive input, "the target language that learners are exposed to, but do not respond to verbally" (p. 143), and interactive input, which "arises from the social interactions that a learner participates in with other people—either other learners or native speakers" (p. 145). Students do not engage with all the input in or out of the classroom, and our focus is on the input that students are exposed to in their ESL/EFL courses.

Gass and Mackey (2015) argue that "input is an essential component for learning in that it provides the crucial evidence from which learners can form linguistic hypotheses" (p. 182). This evidence may be *positive*, well-formed examples of structures and meanings that are possible in English, or *negative*, such as information about what is not possible grammatically or semantically in English or the correction of what doesn't match English norms (and is thus wrong). Gass, Behney, and Plonsky (2013) declare, "There is some empirical evidence that negative evidence is, in some instances, necessary for SLA" (p. 360).

REFLECTIVE QUESTIONS

- Please take a moment to reflect on one of your classes. What are the important sources of English input in your class?

- Next you might consider whether the input in your course is positive, negative, or both, and whether your students are typically interacting with this input in specific ways.

Hopefully, teachers gear the level of input toward their students' English proficiency level and use examples, texts, and other input that is at, and slightly more difficult than, their students' level. Students neither grasp all input nor "learn" everything that is taught in an ESL/EFL class. Ellis and Shintani (2014) observe that much learning takes place through incidental input and that "some level of comprehension of the input is required for acquisition to take place," yet forms noticed in the input "are more likely to be acquired than those that are not noticed" (p. 187). So helping learners pay attention to input is important in SLA.

The above issues are essential for teachers to consider because rich classroom input helps students learn English, but learners also need to "pay attention to linguistic forms in the input that they have not yet acquired" (Ellis & Shintani, 2014, p. 190). Thus grammar, vocabulary, pronunciation, spelling, and other features of English can be learned as they are linked to meaning and become comprehensible to learners. Simplified English may be appropriate, and often seems to aid comprehension, but simplifying one's speech or writing doesn't necessarily mean that students will understand it. The type of input students receive is key, because Lightbown and Spada (2013) declare that classroom learners typically "spend less time in contact with the new language," are often "taught language that is somewhat formal in comparison to the language as it is used in most social settings," and "tend to be exposed to a far smaller range of discourse types" than ESL students in natural learning environments (p. 39).

REFLECTIVE QUESTIONS

Consider the English input in your course.

- What is the balance between oral and written input?

- Do you tend to simplify your speech and writing in class?

- Do you use examples on the board or in a PowerPoint presentation, while reading them aloud to appeal to auditory learners and visual learners?

The Linguistic System and Input

Renandya (2013) succinctly notes that ESL/EFL students are interested in developing both the underlying linguistic system of English and the ability to use this system for communication. The linguistic system of English includes the lexicon (the vocabulary—words and phrases), phonology (the sound system reflected in pronunciation and speech recognition), syntax (the grammar and rules governing sentence structure), discourse (the ability to produce longer stretches of speech and writing), and pragmatics (the system enabling people to interpret meaning and produce culturally appropriate language). In SLA, input is crucial to developing knowledge and use of this underlying linguistic system, while output and interaction help students refine their ability to use all of these components.

As noted in Chapter 2, Krashen's (2003) "input hypothesis claims . . . that comprehending messages is the only way language is acquired" (p. 4). Krashen thus promotes the importance of extensive reading (ER), which develops good reading habits while increasing students' knowledge of English grammar and vocabulary. ER "is also a source of input for developing L2 proficiency, especially vocabulary" (Ellis & Shintani, 2014, p. 171). Recent research suggests that for vocabulary learning in particular, extensive reading while also listening to what is being read (e.g., through audiobooks) is an effective way for students to have access to simultaneous written and aural input, whether in or out of the English language class.

REFLECTIVE QUESTIONS

Now look back at your list of input sources in your course.

- What aspects of the linguistic system does this input emphasize (e.g., grammar, lexis, pronunciation)?

- How do you help students pay attention to this input and learn to use it?

- Are there additional ways that you can help students notice it?

Loewen (2015) argues that input alone is not necessarily useful until it becomes intake, the actual language that students incorporate into their own L2 speaking, writing, and so on. "Thus, intake is defined as that part of the input that is noticed, comprehended, and taken in to the cognitive system" (p. 41). In brief, intake involves those aspects of the linguistic system that learners are able to hold and process in their working memory, and it usually begins with content words and expands as one gains more knowledge of English to include many of the various aspects of the linguistic system introduced above. As H. D. Brown (2014) observes, students typically take in "only a fraction of language that is perceived," so maximizing quality input in our classes is important (pp. 262–263). But doing so is often connected to output.

CHAPTER 4

SLA Essential II: Output

Input is not enough in second language acquisition. English language teaching also requires appropriate output.

Output

Output is the language that learners produce, whether in speech or in writing. Yet VanPatten (2003) writes that, more specifically, "*output* in SLA means language that has a *communicative purpose*" (p. 62, original emphasis). Teachers know that students can repeat after others and produce target language utterances, but VanPatten argues that true output is for communication, whether in oral interaction or through e-mail or other writings. This is a useful distinction. However, while teaching in China I remember that many Chinese students often memorized famous speeches in English that they would recite orally, in speaking practice on campus or at local English corners. What I observed among my students is that those who regularly practised English in this way also tended to have better pronunciation and oral communication skills. So perhaps reciting a speech in English to oneself in front of the mirror or for an audience is a useful output exercise for pronunciation practice and oral skills development, even if it doesn't clearly meet VanPatten's communicative purpose criterion.

REFLECTIVE QUESTION

- What activities in your class enable students to produce output with a clear communicative purpose? Think of specific tasks and purposes.

In studying L2 learners in French immersion classes in Canada, Merrill Swain (1993) developed the *output hypothesis*, largely in response to and in order to complement Krashen's (2003) input hypothesis. Although immersion students received much comprehensible input and often exhibited confidence in communicating in French, they didn't always display good grammatical competence. Swain thus argued that input alone is not enough and that students' limited and often minimal output did not require them to produce more accurate, complex, and precise French utterances. She thus used the phrase *pushed output* to describe the type of output that required such learners to use correct, appropriate French in interactions.

Swain (1993) suggested that such pushed output has four main purposes that assist in L2 learning. First, it gives learners chances for meaningful language practice, well beyond simple utterances. Second, it helps students move from semantic to syntactic processing, because in such output they need to go beyond meaning in communication to oral or written accuracy in order to succeed in communicating. Third, pushed output provides opportunities for students to develop and test hypotheses about the target language system and to then adjust or modify their output based on feedback from others with whom they are interacting. Fourth, pushed output generates responses from others that students then interact with, which can in turn help them (re)process their own output. If, for example, a student says something they believe is clear but the person they are talking to cannot understand what they meant, then the student may modify what they said or wrote and try again, often with communicative success.

Functions of Output in SLA

Later, Swain (2005) introduced three main functions of output in SLA. First is that learners "notice that they do not know how to say (or write) precisely the meaning they wish to convey" (p. 474). Students' attention is thus focused on their need to discover something specific about the grammar, vocabulary, pronunciation, and other elements of what they want to communicate. Here Swain notes that "grammatical encoding is quite different in its effect from grammatical decoding, which does not push learners to reorganize their form-meaning mappings" (p. 476). So output helps students notice aspects of their SLA and pushes them further in developing their underlying linguistic system.

Second, Swain (2005) reiterated the hypothesis testing function of output, which she suggested gives students "a 'trial run' reflecting their hypothesis of how to say (or write) their intent" (p. 476). When trying to determine how to say or write what they mean, students are thus reflecting "the processes in which learners engage to modify their output in response to feedback" (p. 476). The third function is a metalinguistic one, where students use output to reflect consciously on the target language forms that communicate their meaning. "The claim here is that using language to reflect on language produced by others or the self . . . mediates second language learning" (p. 478). Swain suggests this happens naturally when learners use output to negotiate meaning and face communication problems during communicative tasks.

If you have difficulty thinking of specific tasks that do these three things in your class, then you may want to consider adjusting your teaching and creating opportunities to allow for productive, pushed output activities where students can experience these benefits.

Conclusion

As we have seen, output connects with many aspects of input. One student's output in a pair or small-group activity becomes input for others with whom they are interacting. In pair or group tasks students need to work together in order to solve communication problems; this not only helps them pay attention to meaning, but also may enable them to notice linguistic forms. Unlike input, which is largely receptive, output involves speech or writing that requires increased depth of processing, using long-term memory, as does interaction, to which we turn next.

CHAPTER 5

SLA Essential III: Interaction

With appropriate input and output, one is on the right track in English language teaching. Yet a third essential in second language acquisition is interaction.

Interaction

Building on work in input and output, Michael Long's (1996) *interaction hypothesis* agreed that comprehensible input is necessary for SLA, but added that modified interaction makes such input comprehensible, where students negotiate for meaning and reach mutual comprehension. Such modified interaction might not just involve simplification, but through breakdowns in communication would require comprehension checks, contextual cues, elaboration, repetition or paraphrase, or requests for clarification during classroom interaction. In developing this hypothesis, Long suggested that cognitive factors such as noticing or corrective feedback in interaction help students when communication is not easy. Interaction thus offers students the opportunity for modified input and output through the negotiation of meaning.

Loewen (2015) summarizes the empirical evidence on interaction: "There are multiple individual studies, as well as meta-analyses, that have found interaction in the classroom to be beneficial for L2 development" (p. 50). Further, "communicative interaction can have a positive effect on L2 acquisition," yet "not all interaction is successful in all contexts" (p. 52). As a result, Loewen proposes several pedagogical implications. First, he indicates the importance of bringing "communicative tasks into the classroom" that allow for the exchange and negotiation of meaning (p. 52). Second, such activities should allow for the pushed output outlined in Chapter 4, providing opportunities for students to communicate in the target language, which is "important for the development of implicit knowledge, procedural knowledge, and communicative competence" (p. 53). Third, teachers in second or foreign language contexts should tell students "the benefits of peer interaction" and educate them on "how to recognize learning opportunities during interaction and how to seek and provide communicative assistance" (p. 53).

REFLECTIVE QUESTIONS

- How do you encourage interaction among students in your class? What benefits of communicative interaction do you highlight for students?

In many ELT contexts teachers have classes of 40 to 50 (or more) students, and they may rightly wonder if it is really possible to incorporate interaction into such courses. Yet with clear directions and modelling, in my experience it is possible. For example, while working for over a decade in Japan, I taught an English listening skills course with 40 to 50 students in each section. In order to go beyond the textbook and other listening materials and to allow for mixed input and output among students, I used pair work and occasionally small-group work in every class, including brainstorming, exchanges of ideas and opinions, information gap tasks, and so on. These activities came from both our text as well as handouts and prompts on the board. I worked with students so they learned to see one another as potential sources of input and interaction.

According to Loewen (2015), a range of activities, including discussions, games, information gaps, and role-plays, helps students interact with one another in class, often after considering "examples of authentic L1 interaction" (p. 53). Models are great, yet teachers need to move students beyond simple repetition to enabling them to negotiate for meaning in class as much as possible. As Benati and Angelovska (2016) explain, "Output practice should help learners to use the target language for a specific purpose and intent rather than simply learning by rote" (p. 12). Interaction thus requires negotiation involving both input and output—much more than students simply reciting famous speeches in English!

REFLECTIVE QUESTIONS

- What activities in your class enable students to produce modified input and output? How can they help students truly negotiate in interaction?

Types of Interaction

Given that interactions with native English speakers may well be different than with students' peers, Loewen (2015) believes it is "important to consider what types of possibilities there are to encourage learners to engage with L2 speakers outside of the classroom" (p. 54). An example of this comes from one of my graduate students who teaches English in a tourist city in Japan. She prepares her high school students in class with the English input and practice useful for output in order for them to conduct short surveys with people from other countries visiting the city. This teacher then helps her students engage in face-to-face interaction with native and nonnative English speakers in English about tourist sites and the visitors' comments on and opinions of them. While this type of interaction is not possible in every context, Loewen suggests computer-mediated communication is another option, and I know of teachers who have used key pals for their students to experience different types of written interaction practice.

In these types of interactions, students need to ask for clarification, check their understanding, negotiate meaning, and so on, all of which provide opportunities for the communication of meaning, noticing, and L2 learning. As Benati and Angelovska (2016) summarize, "Conversation and interaction make linguistic features salient to learners and therefore increase their chances of acquisition" (p. 141). Arguing "the more interaction, the better," VanPatten (2003, p. 108) encourages teachers to move beyond interaction with students in their classes to engage students in various level-appropriate tasks with one another, where students themselves help manage and perhaps modify their input and output. In short, input and output come together in interaction, supporting ESL/EFL students' SLA.

Here are some specific ways to encourage interaction in English language classes and to support appropriate input and output:

- Clearly explain and model the benefits of peer interaction to students.

- Allow enough time in class for activities and tasks to enable students' pushed output and the modified interaction discussed above.

- Teach students in class how to bridge communication breakdowns in pair work.

- Use prompts to help students offer one another feedback in interaction, especially when something communicated is unclear or not understood.

REFLECTIVE QUESTION

- How could you incorporate these options to encourage and enable better interaction among students in a specific class you teach?

Conclusion

This chapter introduced interaction as an essential SLA topic in order to help English language teachers understand and reflect on the importance and roles of input, output, and interaction in ELT. Please consider the following vignette and reflect on the questions that follow.

Vignette 1: Teaching College ESL

Joe teaches intermediate ESL at a community college in Toronto, Canada, a diverse international city. He has 20 students from different language/cultural backgrounds, including many from Asia, Europe, and Central America. Students range in age, and most are learning English so they can attend university, be exempted from further ESL courses, or apply for certification in their professions. Joe helps learners improve their English proficiency, yet some students skip class, saying they're too busy studying for the TOEFL to regularly attend class.

Joe uses a current, four skills textbook that helps students review important English grammar and vocabulary, and use oral and written skills. His students do extensive reading and use vocabulary learning strategies to expand and practise their lexical knowledge. Joe works hard to ensure a good balance in his classes between input, output, and interaction among students.

REFLECTIVE QUESTIONS

- What are three positive things Joe does in his course? How does his teaching seem appropriate for his students? How might you learn from his approach?

- What sources of input do you observe? Opportunities for output? Interaction? What might you say to Joe's students who regularly miss class?

Age, Anxiety, and Error Correction in SLA and ELT

This chapter offers an overview of three important issues in second or foreign language learning—age, anxiety, and error correction—and how these topics can impact students' second language acquisition.

Age and SLA

According to Strid (2017), "the belief that children have a language learning advantage is widespread in general culture," with adults considered at a major disadvantage in L2/FL learning (p. 700). S. Brown and Larson-Hall (2012) call this a myth: "Children learn languages quickly and easily while adults are ineffective in comparison" (p. 1). This view is due to the *critical period hypothesis* (CPH), which states that there is "a narrow . . . window of opportunity for optimal language learning, and this period usually extends only to about puberty," around 12 years old (Scovel, 2001, p. 113). After three decades studying it, Scovel (2001) has concluded that "exceptions to the CPH are exceedingly rare and that virtually all learners (not just a simple majority of learners) experience critical period constraints in their second language performance" (p. 113).

Scovel (2001) summarizes three main positions on this topic, the first being that there is a critical period, but that it's confined only to L2/FL accent: "Given all the right conditions, anyone can acquire the phonology of any language like a native before about the age of 12" (p. 114). This is Scovel's view, that "the CPH only holds for foreign accents and is probably accounted for by neurological factors" (p. 114). The second position is that there is a critical period not only for accents, but also for syntax. Using grammaticality judgements for articles *a*/*the* and third person –*s*, studies suggest that there are maturational constraints on learning the fine details of syntax. Some SLA researchers believe this to be the case, but Scovel is not convinced. The third position is that some authors argue that there is no critical period, not even for pronunciation (p. 115). This view is reflected in some research, but Scovel rightly notes problems with many older studies, stating that some native speakers' pronunciation was rated as nonnative!

My experience with ESL/EFL students around the world indicates that there is clearly some evidence for positions 1 and 2, and any exceptions to the rule (and there are many) explain position 3. Given that teachers cannot change their students' ages, however, I don't believe that overall this is a crucial issue. The CPH is largely focused on accent and naturalistic ESL settings. Yet most SLA takes place in L2/FL classrooms, and Spada (2015) reminds us that for instructed ESL/EFL learning, "school contexts favor older learners, because of their superior cognitive development and the advantages provided by their explicit learning mechanisms" (p. 74). Students need to know that intelligibility is more important in communication than accent. I also agree with Pfenninger and Singleton (2017) that the obsession with the "'earlier = better' myth" simply ignores the reality that "real empirical evidence of long-term advantages emerging under such conditions is in fact not available" (p. 211).

As introduced in Chapter 1, teachers should consider what they and their students bring to L2/FL learning: Children appear to learn best implicitly, while adults draw on a great deal of language and life experience, and thus explicit examples are usually most helpful to them. Another key point from S. Brown and Larson-Hall (2012) concerns "realistic expectations for how long it takes . . . to learn a language" (p. 18). Although research suggests adults can learn more quickly, "learning languages requires time, effort, and perseverance, but success is certainly possible and is not constrained by a critical period" (Strid, 2017, p. 710).

It's important for teachers to teach in ways that will best help students learn. And we need to help learners have realistic expectations of the time and effort required to learn English well.

Anxiety and L2 Learning

As outlined in Chapter 2, Krashen's (2003) affective filter hypothesis argues that negative variables block input and impede SLA, and a key issue in L2/FL learning is anxiety. According to Gregersen and MacIntyre (2014), "Language anxiety reflects the worry and negative emotional reaction aroused when learning and using a second language and is especially relevant in a classroom where self-expression takes place" (p. 3). If one teaches for input, output, and interaction, then they should expect self-expression and thus some student anxiety.

Research has distinguished trait anxiety, defined as a generally "permanent predisposition to be anxious" (H. D. Brown, 2014, p. 150), and state anxiety, which is the result of particular situations rather than a student's individual personality. In L2/FL classes, students have various opportunities to feel anxious, including "communication apprehension" as they struggle to express important beliefs and thoughts in the target language, the "fear of negative social evaluation" by and among their classroom peers, and "test anxiety, or apprehension over academic evaluation" (H. D. Brown, 2014, p. 151). This latter category in state anxiety can be impacted by error correction, for example, which we consider briefly below.

In English we tend to view anxiety as negative, as Krashen's (2003) concerns about the affective filter do. In such a case L2 anxiety can be debilitating, when learners are so uncomfortable in class for some reason that they are unable to process input or contribute output, and thus there is a clear, negative impact on their L2 learning. Yet others, such as Spielmann and Radnofsky (2001), have suggested the more neutral term *tension* and distinguish between affective tension (dealing with students' emotions) and cognitive tension (related to students' mental capacities and thinking). While affective tension or anxiety can be debilitating, Spielmann and Radnofsky argue that cognitive tension may be facilitative anxiety and thus a positive factor in SLA. Facilitative anxiety can help keep students alert and offer them just enough tension to accomplish a task, as when one is slightly nervous before a presentation or test and does well.

REFLECTIVE QUESTIONS

- Do you notice any types of anxiety among students in your classes?

- What steps might you take to reduce any potentially debilitating anxiety? What steps might you take to encourage your students to work with any positive, facilitative anxiety?

In L2/FL teaching, teachers can work to reduce students' state anxiety by ensuring that activities and materials are at the right level of difficulty for their classes and by "scrutinizing their classroom procedures for anxiety triggers" (Gregersen & MacIntyre, 2014, p. 11). Creating a comfortable class atmosphere where students feel free to make mistakes and know that they will be encouraged and rewarded for their efforts can work wonders in reducing debilitating anxiety in one's classes. Creating a less stressful ESL/EFL class environment by addressing students' expectations is also important. This may be done through verbal communication (e.g., appropriate praise) as well as through nonverbal attention, smiles, and warmth. Yet another option is to train students in strategies for minimizing L2 anxiety. Gregersen and MacIntyre (2014), for example, offer 15 anxiety-reducing activities. To limit test anxiety, teachers can ensure that students do not face any surprises on exams and that they are never asked to do something in an assessment that they have not already had several opportunities to practise, with feedback, in class or for homework.

Especially for adult learners, it's important to remember that students and classes also bear some responsibility for managing classroom anxiety, as with other aspects of SLA. Teachers therefore need to make students aware of issues in L2 anxiety and help both individual students and classes prepare, think positively, and use whatever individual or peer support strategies that will help them have a positive, lower anxiety ESL/EFL learning experience.

Error Correction in ELT

If teachers provide rich English language input, opportunities for pushed output, and class interaction, as suggested in Chapters 3 through 5, then they will naturally encounter student errors. The first point here is that this is absolutely normal and should be expected in L2/FL learning. If students don't make mistakes then they won't learn English, as mistakes are part and parcel of English language learning. So dealing with student errors is an important job for teachers in order to push learners to notice gaps in their linguistic knowledge and in their oral and written English output. In important ways, error correction is a specific type of input students receive that can help them perceive such gaps between their knowledge and their English language performance.

H. D. Brown (2014) offers a helpful distinction between *mistakes*, which are slips that reflect learners' inability to use what they know of the language, and *errors*, which occur when students really don't know what is correct, and thus their English use reflects a gap in their linguistic competence. Gass, Behney, and Plonsky (2013) argue that positive input alone is insufficient, and thus negative evidence, through explicit error correction, is important in SLA in order for students to notice the gaps in their understanding of English and its use. Let's remind students that they can learn from their mistakes, which is why teachers encourage students to feel comfortable to make mistakes, even as we correct students and help them learn to correct themselves as they notice aspects of their English speech and writing that need improvement.

The reality is that teachers simply cannot correct every error a student makes, even if that were desirable. H. D. Brown (2014) also distinguishes between *global* errors that clearly impede communication and more *local* ones that do not, because with the latter, usually the error truly is a slip or the person listening or reading can easily guess what is meant. Global errors, which impede spoken or written communication, are primary and require attention, especially if the pronunciation, spelling, or usage will communicate something very different from what the speaker or writer intends. Various authors offer different direct (e.g., writing the correct form or word directly above) or indirect correction (e.g., underlining a problem word, structure, etc.). In written work in particular, many teachers use coding systems, such as *SVA = subject verb agreement*. Research is clear that a key point is to correct errors in learners' spoken or written English in explicit ways that help them notice and learn from such errors. Isolated correction is not usually effective if teachers correct a student but do not give explicit attention to the specific error.

REFLECTIVE QUESTIONS

- How useful do you think the mistakes/errors and global/local distinctions are? How might you use them in correcting your students?

- How explicit and systematic is your correction? Do students notice it?

There are many types of corrective feedback that teachers can offer students, including clarification prompts (e.g., Sorry, I didn't understand what you said.), repetition, and recasts (e.g., S: Yesterday I go downtown. T: Oh, you *went* downtown yesterday?). Research indicates that these and other corrective feedback strategies can be effective. Lightbown and Spada (2013, p. 139), for example, emphasize the positive role of recasts in oral error correction, which is one of the most common teacher strategies. In an interesting study involving a foreign EFL teacher using recasts with individual students in Japan, Sato (2009) determined that recasts were more effective when they were short (five or fewer morphemes) and/or involved only one change (rather than those that incorporated multiple corrections). Often less is more, and students can recognize and incorporate teachers' corrective feedback when it is brief and explicit. Yet teachers also need to be aware of students' expectations for error correction and adjust to their needs if possible.

In class, spoken errors often occur in the context of interpersonal communication where clarification questions may be asked or nonverbal communication can signal to a student that someone cannot comprehend their speech. Like native and nonnative English speakers interacting with English learners, if they get the gist then often teachers will let mistakes pass in conversation. Yet written errors are more permanent and may be responded to in class over time. Accordingly, it may be most helpful for teachers to let students know what errors they will focus on and then to be consistent in that for a particular activity, composition, presentation, or task.

REFLECTIVE QUESTIONS

- How can you help students notice gaps in their knowledge of and production in English? What explicit feedback might you offer them?

A final comment about error correction is that it should ideally be part of a teacher's larger plan for feedback to students, and such feedback should focus not only on problems. Students are human beings who appreciate encouragement when they try some new structure or vocabulary and praise when they do something well, particularly in their output and interaction in class. When was the last time you told a student, "Bravo! Great job!"? Depending on the context, a smile, a high five, or a pat on the back may be the best form of positive feedback to offer. Teachers can even approach error correction with a positive take. One of my former graduate students, for example, often tells her students, "Great mistake!" when they say or write something wrong. She then goes on to explain how the error reflects their growing knowledge of English but misses the mark in some way, detailing the correct way to communicate what they mean. This teacher shows students that she values their mistakes as opportunities for them to use their English and for her to see the positive ways they are growing in their linguistic competence.

Conclusion

While teachers cannot do much about their students' age, they can work to reduce anxiety in class and to use error correction techniques that will not only help create a positive learning environment but also help students notice gaps and work to improve their English use.

CHAPTER 7

Using Materials That Reflect SLA Principles

As introduced in Chapter 3, textbooks and other materials are major sources of input in English language teaching. If we wish to capitalize on these for students' second language acquisition, then we need to use materials that support L2 learning. Tomlinson (2017) offers five principles for language learning that can help teachers achieve a match between SLA theory and ELT materials.

Recycle Rich and Meaningful Input

Tomlinson's (2017) first principle is "that the learners are exposed to a rich, re-cycled, meaningful and comprehensible input of language in use" (p. 7). While drawing on aspects of input from Chapter 3, this principle connects it to repetition and recycling in our materials in order to provide input that is both comprehensible and meaningful to students. Reusing and recycling grammar and vocabulary is key because Nation (2013) argues students often need to interact with a word or phrase 10 or more times in order to learn it. So it's not enough to provide input; the input in class should be rich in ways outlined here, recycled for better comprehension, and meaningful to students so they can connect with the content in their specific context.

Engage Learners Both Affectively and Cognitively

The second principle that Tomlinson (2017) offers is "that the learners are affectively engaged" (p. 8), and this draws directly from Krashen's (2003) affective filter hypothesis. Tomlinson argues that students need to engage with the topics and content of learning materials, and thus these materials need to be interesting, not "bland, neutral texts and uninvolving activities" that prevent language learning. Yet students should not only "feel" in relation to our materials and classes, as the next principle from Tomlinson is "that learners are cognitively engaged" (p. 8). As Tomlinson puts it, "If they are involved in challenging but achievable tasks which require high-level, critical and creative thinking, learners are much more likely to move towards language acquisition than if they are mindlessly repeating drills, or . . . reading empty texts" (p. 8).

REFLECTIVE QUESTIONS

- In what specific ways does your text/teaching material recycle vocabulary and grammar? How is the content especially meaningful?

- Does the material offer interesting connections that engage learners affectively and cognitively? If not, what can be done to do so?

Help Learners Notice Form and Meaning

Tomlinson's (2017) fourth principle is "that the learners are sometimes helped to pay attention to form whilst or after focusing on meaning" (p. 8). Meaning is essential to effective communication, but form can alter or distort such meaning. In order for Krashen's (2003) Monitor hypothesis to be applied effectively, students need to be aware of form and correctness, know the rule, and have time to think about these particular things. Tomlinson's suggestion is for "a language awareness approach in which learners make discoveries for themselves about language features of texts which they have experienced" (p. 9).

Give Students Opportunities to Use the Language

Tomlinson's (2017) fifth principle states "that the learners are given plentiful opportunities to use the language for communication" (p. 9). Here Swain's (2005) pushed output is essential, as is contextual interaction with other students that enables "meaningful communication in the sense that it stimulates the expression of views, opinions, reactions, intentions" and not just simple answers (Tomlinson, 2017, p. 9).

REFLECTIVE QUESTIONS

- In what ways does your material help students notice form and meaning?

- What different types of opportunities does the text provide for students to use the language productively in interaction? Be specific.

Conclusion

Teachers work in various contexts where they have absolute freedom to choose or create their own materials, and in other situations where they have to use a specific text and supplementing it is discouraged. The ideal is to use ELT materials that offer rich and meaningful input, engage students both affectively and cognitively, help them notice form as they address meaning in English, and do so as they are involved in varied opportunities for interaction. If one's textbook and other materials do not do this, a major option is to supplement and/or adapt them so that they engage students and challenge them in interaction beyond their current level. As Tomlinson (2017) indicates, if one's text asks only for a time or day, for example, one should follow up with discussions of students' views and opinions concerning those options.

REFLECTIVE QUESTIONS

- Choose a unit in your current textbook. Analyze it using Tomlinson's (2017) five principles. How does it fare? What does it do well? How would you need to supplement this unit in order to truly promote English language learning?

Putting It Together: What SLA Offers Classroom Teachers

This chapter answers the question of what second language acquisition offers classroom ESL/EFL teachers. It outlines five points and suggests implications for each of these benefits of SLA for teachers.

A Reality Check on the Complexity of Language Learning

As I hope this short book has revealed, SLA is complicated. A recent survey article by Tarone (2015) bears this out, as do more thorough treatments of second language acquisition by Benati and Angelovska (2016), Cook (2016), Ellis (2015), Loewen (2015), and Loewen and Sato (2017). Second or foreign language learning is extremely complex (VanPatten, 2017) and involves many different factors, including first language issues and language transfer, the role of culture, communicative competence, and numerous challenges pertaining to language learning (H. D. Brown, 2014).

As teachers know, students learn as individuals, and individual differences in SLA are numerous. Dörnyei and Ryan's (2015) overview, for example, considers personality traits, language aptitude, motivation, learning styles and cognitive styles, language learning strategies and self-regulation, and other learner characteristics, such as anxiety, creativity, self-esteem, and willingness to communicate, all of which should be considered. Often it seems one's rate of L2/FL learning is clearly connected to individual differences.

The implication here is that both teachers and students need to be aware of the complexity of L2/FL learning, and an important teacher role is to help students understand this complexity and what they can do to learn best. As S. Brown and Larson-Hall (2012) make crystal clear, most people have strong opinions about language learning, and there are many myths surrounding SLA in particular. As teachers learn about SLA and its complexity, it is important that they educate their students about the realities of L2 learning—both the challenges and the blessings. The fact is that children take many years to learn their L1, and adolescents and adults also require time to effectively acquire an L2/FL. In sum, SLA offers teachers a reality check on the complexity of both what students are going through in ESL/EFL classes and what teachers can do as they work effectively to teach English.

REFLECTIVE QUESTIONS

- What is one important point you have noted about the complexity of SLA? How might you share about it with your ESL/EFL students?

A Reminder Regarding Appropriate Input, Output, and Interaction

Research on L2/FL learning and instruction reveals that learners need both rich and varied input in the target language and opportunities to use the language (VanPatten, 2003), as we saw in Chapters 3 through 5. Input is indeed key, but research by Mackey (2008) and others reveals the importance of output and interaction as well. Swain (1993) argued that output offers students meaningful language practice, helps them go beyond semantic to syntactic processing, provides opportunities for developing and testing hypotheses, and creates responses to interact with from others that can help them process their own output. In discussing collaborative dialogue, Swain,

Kinnear, and Steinman (2015) suggest teachers help students go beyond transmitting information to collaboration through having them engage in important (not trivial) content and topics, and by encouraging them to be creative with language, to try out "old and new forms and see what meanings they are able to create with these forms, and . . . to reflect on this process" (p. 42).

Gass and Mackey (2015) similarly build on input and output in outlining their interactionist approach, noting that both positive and negative feedback are important components in students' L2/FL learning. The implication here is that teachers need to provide students with rich input in class, opportunities for output (written and spoken), and interaction in practice, plus feedback on their L2/FL use (what they do well and what they need to improve). Whatever class they teach, ELT instructors must teach in ways that incorporate such valuable input, output, and interaction to foster students' SLA. Please read the following vignette, consider the options, and then answer the questions about it.

Vignette 2: Input, Output, and Interaction in SLA

Akiko teaches EFL to undergraduates from various majors at a university in Japan. Some students in her required listening class expect to hear English only from native English speakers, but their textbook uses example conversations between nonnative English speakers as well as others between native and nonnative English speakers, both in English-dominant countries and other contexts.

In Akiko's writing course learners want to study academic writing, yet they struggle with communicating clearly and efficiently in anything other than simple sentences. She wonders how to help her students grasp the realities of English in the 21st century for both oral and written communication. Beyond her textbooks, she would like to incorporate real-world examples of oral/aural communication and useful written texts that learners will encounter beyond their EFL courses.

While there are many possible options in this scenario, it's important for Akiko's students to understand that English is used by many people throughout the world to communicate for business or personal reasons with other nonnative English speakers. By including topics and conversations relevant to her students' interests, she could prepare them for various types of listening passages through pair work brainstorming possibilities and follow up after they complete such exercises with "Now Over to You!" opportunities for interaction on those particular issues, as Tomlinson (2017) suggests. Similarly, in the writing class Akiko might incorporate lessons on more complex sentences and paragraphs, but also show how simple phrases are used in English e-mails and text messages that students can use in communicating with key pals in other contexts.

A Balanced Perspective on Vocabulary, Grammar, and Focus on Form

Partly in response to Krashen's (2003) work, Laufer's (2003) study asked whether learners actually acquire vocabulary most through reading. She compared reading alone versus productive tasks (using glosses, writing sentences, writing a composition, sentence completion) in Israeli EFL classes. In all cases the empirical evidence suggested (in relation to vocabulary) that a word's meaning is more likely to be remembered in a "productive word-focused task" than simply through reading, even when the word is looked up in a dictionary (p. 581). This key finding with several class experiments and statistical significance clearly suggests that the benefits of English instruction are not limited to form and/or grammar, but include vocabulary learning, and that both input and output are valuable. In answer to Krashen, then, free voluntary reading is indeed useful, but it does not seem to be enough, especially in the EFL classroom.

While there are various views on form-focused instruction (FFI; e.g., Spada, 2011), SLA suggests some FFI is important to learners' L2/FL development. Byrd (2005) summarizes issues on instructed grammar and suggests planning ahead for focus on form, using recasts effectively, and recognizing grammar in context. The implications here are that teachers need to recognize the importance of grammar as well as vocabulary (Nation, 2013) and include relevant FFI when there may be a problem, perhaps by planning lessons to anticipate such issues with form, and deal with it in as unobtrusive a manner as possible. Spada (2011) concludes that "there is increasing evidence that instruction, including explicit FFI, can positively contribute to unanalyzed spontaneous production," and it is not "restricted to controlled/analyzed L2 knowledge" (p. 233). In sum, FFI and useful error correction are helpful to students in their SLA and are likely to help them notice what to change or improve in their speaking and writing.

REFLECTIVE QUESTIONS

- In what ways do you balance vocabulary and grammar teaching?

- How do you highlight form in teaching to assist your students' learning?

- What additional methods can you use to incorporate useful error correction?

Suggestions for What to Focus on in Teaching

Much research and theory is hard to connect with classroom learning and teaching. Yet often SLA articles include "implications for teaching" that teachers can evaluate in relation to the applicability of any such suggestions for their particular contexts.

Nation (2013) offers an interesting perspective on the role of the teacher in classroom contexts, stating that to teach is only one of the instructor's four main jobs, with the other three being to plan appropriate lessons, to train students in language skills, and to test their progress. In his framework for instruction, Nation argues four strands are necessary: meaning-focused input, meaning-focused output, deliberate language study, and fluency development.

Some implications of these perspectives are to include a range of activities in classes to allow students to practise and develop their English skills through meaning-focused input and output, specific language study skills, and fluency practice. Yet we should also recognize that the focus in language classes should be on learners and their goals, not teachers or the curriculum.

REFLECTIVE QUESTIONS

- How much of your class time is spent on meaning-focused input, output, language-focused activities, and fluency practice? Be specific. (Nation, 2013, recommends one quarter for each.) Should you rebalance these?

Encouragement, Since Classroom Instruction Helps L2 Learning

Long (1983) attempted to review research on instruction compared with L2 exposure, focused on Krashen's (2003) acquisition versus instruction distinction. In terms of varying amount of instruction versus exposure, Long concluded instruction was beneficial; however, it was clear that there were major problems in making such comparisons, often due to a lack of information in published research, different definitions of SLA, and so on. In a later attempt to consider whether instruction makes a difference, Long (1988) studied four domains of SLA: processes (transfer, generalization, noticing, etc.), route (developmental sequences in negation, questions, word order, etc.), rate (speed of learning), and level of ultimate attainment. Doughty (2003, pp. 261–263) offers a brief summary of Long's (1988) findings:

- In terms of SLA processes, findings indicate that there are both similarities and differences in naturalistic learning and L2/FL learning in classroom settings. In short, learning processes must be understood in order to enhance SLA in any learning context.

- As for SLA route, developmental sequences exist and can be influenced by the learner's L1. Like students in immersion settings, L2 learners in the classroom can't skip developmental stages of language learning and must be ready for instruction.

- In relation to SLA rate of acquisition, Long noted several studies showed a rate advantage for instructed classroom learners. Thus Long suggested rightly timed instruction "can speed SLA."

- For SLA attainment, Long observed advantages for instructed learners, noting that L2/FL instruction can help develop communicative competence.

While not conclusive, the evidence clearly indicates that instruction can help L2 learning.

Norris and Ortega (2000) later surveyed 250 possibly relevant studies related to the effectiveness of L2 instruction and were able to screen 77 that met their (quasi-)experimental focus on L2 features, but then only 49 reported adequate statistical data to be included in their meta-analysis. They observed some 20 pedagogical procedures (instructional treatments) in the remaining studies that concerned five variables (two on the type of instruction: explicit vs. implicit; three on attention to form: focus mainly on meaning, form, or forms). While they couldn't comment on the different instructional types, Norris and Ortega concluded that "L2 instruction can be characterized as effective in its own right, at least as operationalized and measured within the domain" (p. 480). L2 instruction can be effective!

In critiquing Norris and Ortega's (2000) analysis, Krashen (2003) noted that the comparison groups examined for their study didn't have exposure to the target rules and therefore "they were not in an acquisition-rich environment" (p. 45). Krashen concluded: "Thus, these studies really compare the presence and absence of formal instruction, not acquisition versus learning" (p. 45). The Long (1988) and Norris and Ortega (2000) studies used quantitative and experimental approaches to instructed SLA research and observed the importance of replication studies to support the importance of L2 instruction. More recently, a broader language socialization and SLA perspective has noted that language learning is always "situated and attentionally and socially gated" (Douglas Fir Group, 2016, p. 27). This SLA framework is more descriptive and takes into consideration diverse social, cultural, and learning issues and contexts, recognizing the role of culture in L2 learning and teaching (Lessard-Clouston, 2016).

In essence, *teaching can make a difference to L2 learning*, and the difference appears to be substantial. This research finding is important, because most English language learning takes place in formal or classroom situations around the world, in both ESL and EFL contexts. In discussing the fact that pragmatics are teachable, S. Brown and Larson-Hall (2012) refer to a study and summarize: "Explicit instruction plus lots of opportunities for practice lead to the greatest gains" (p. 148). The same may well be true with other aspects of L2 learning. SLA offers ESL/EFL teachers a range of insights into second language learning and teaching. Perhaps the main value of SLA is to help teachers recognize how understanding *learning* can better inform their *teaching*. Although some experts like Krashen may see little or limited value in formal or classroom language instruction, there is ample evidence in the SLA literature that L2 teaching does make a difference, and I have provided references that discuss that perspective.

Suitable classroom instruction provides ESL/EFL students with (a) useful language models and appropriate input, (b) opportunities to process and practise output in interaction, (c) a focus on relevant form (both grammar and vocabulary), and (d) support and feedback (including through assessment, helpful error correction, etc.). This approach to ELT seems to reflect teachers' "jobs" that Nation (2013) noted as well as his four strands for L2 learning. Echoing the research results, good teaching can and does lead to students' L2 learning!

REFLECTIVE QUESTIONS

- What do you find encouraging about SLA? From your experience, how does good teaching assist students' L2 learning? Enhance it?

Conclusion

SLA is an important field because its research results and theories can help inform classroom teaching. This chapter outlined five points in response to the question of what SLA offers classroom ESL/EFL teachers, dealing with the complexity of L2/FL learning; a reminder of the importance of input, output, and interaction; a balanced view of grammar and vocabulary and the value of form-focused instruction; some suggestions for what to focus on in teaching; and encouragement because research indicates instruction helps students' classroom SLA.

In conclusion, teaching English language learners is a fascinating yet complicated endeavour. Ideally, ESL/EFL teachers not only have a teaching philosophy, but also understand key issues in second language acquisition and are thus able to articulate an understanding of such learning that guides and supports their ELT practice. This short book will not replace a course in SLA (though it might be used as a text in one), but it has introduced a range of views on understanding L2 learning while arguing for a principled yet eclectic approach to SLA (H. D. Brown, 2014). Readers have also been referred to important, relevant research and writings.

I hope the opportunities for reflection here helped you apply specific SLA insights to your context. For additional readings and resources, please refer to the References. All the best as you apply SLA in your English language teaching!

References

Benati, A. G., & Angelovska, T. (2016). *Second language acquisition: A theoretical introduction to real world applications*. London, England: Bloomsbury.

Brown, H. D. (2014). *Principles of language learning and teaching: A course in second language acquisition* (6th ed.). New York, NY: Pearson.

Brown, S., & Larson-Hall, J. (2012). *Second language acquisition myths: Applying second language research to classroom teaching*. Ann Arbor: University of Michigan Press.

Byrd, P. (2005). Instructed grammar. In E. Hinkel (Ed.), *Handbook of research in second language teaching and learning* (pp. 545–561). Mahwah, NJ: Lawrence Erlbaum.

Cook, V. (2016). *Second language learning and language teaching* (5th ed.). London, England: Routledge.

Cook, V., & Li, W. (Eds.). (2016). *The Cambridge handbook of linguistic multi-competence*. Cambridge, England: Cambridge University Press.

De Houwer, A. (2009). *Bilingual first language acquisition*. Bristol, England: Multilingual Matters.

Dörnyei, Z., & Ryan, S. (2015). *The psychology of the language learner revisited*. London, England: Routledge.

Doughty, C. J. (2003). Instructed SLA: Constraints, compensation, and enhancement. In C. J. Doughty & M. H. Long (Eds.), *The handbook of second language acquisition* (pp. 256–310). Oxford, England: Blackwell.

Douglas Fir Group. (2016). A transdisciplinary framework for SLA in a multilingual world. *Modern Language Journal, 100*(S1), 19–47. doi:10.1111/modl.12301

Ellis, R. (2015). *Understanding second language acquisition* (2nd ed.). Oxford, England: Oxford University Press.

Ellis, R., & Shintani, N. (2014). *Exploring language pedagogy through second language acquisition research*. London, England: Routledge.

Farrell, T. S. C. (2017). *Sociolinguistics and language teaching*. Alexandria, VA: TESOL International Association.

Gass, S. M., Behney, J., & Plonsky, L. (2013). *Second language acquisition: An introductory course* (4th ed.). New York, NY: Routledge.

Gass, S. M., & Mackey, A. (2015). Input, interaction, and output in second language acquisition. In B. VanPatten & J. Williams (Eds.), *Theories in second language acquisition: An introduction* (2nd ed., pp. 180–206). London, England: Routledge.

Gregersen, T., & MacIntyre, P. D. (2014). *Capitalizing on language learners' individuality: From premise to practice*. Bristol, England: Multilingual Matters.

Hall, G., & Cook, G. (2014). Own-language use in ELT: Exploring global practices and attitudes Part II. *Language Issues: The ESOL Journal, 25*(2), 39–47.

Krashen, S. D. (2003). *Explorations in language acquisition and use*. Portsmouth, NH: Heinemann.

Laufer, B. (2003). Vocabulary acquisition in a second language: Do learners really acquire most vocabulary by reading? Some empirical evidence. *Canadian Modern Language Review, 59*, 567–587. doi:10.3138/cmlr.59.4.567

Lessard-Clouston, M. (2016). Twenty years of culture learning and teaching research: A survey with highlights and directions. *NECTFL Review, 77*, 53–89.

Lightbown, P. M., & Spada, N. (2013). *How languages are learned* (4th ed.). Oxford, England: Oxford University Press.

Loewen, S. (2015). *Introduction to instructed second language acquisition*. London, England: Routledge.

Loewen, S., & Sato, M. (Eds.). (2017). *The Routledge handbook of instructed second language acquisition*. London, England: Routledge.

Long, M. H. (1983). Does instruction make a difference? *TESOL Quarterly, 17*, 359–382. doi:10.2307/3586253

Long, M. (1988). Instructed interlanguage development. In L. Beebe (Ed.), *Issues in second language acquisition* (pp. 115–141). New York, NY: Newbury House.

Long, M. H. (1996). The role of the linguistic environment in second language acquisition. In W. Ritchie & T. Bhatia (Eds.), *Handbook of second language acquisition* (pp. 413–468). San Diego, CA: Academic Press.

Mackey, A. (Ed.). (2008). *Conversational interaction and second language acquisition: A series of empirical studies*. Cambridge, England: Cambridge University Press.

Nation, I. S. P. (2013). *Learning vocabulary in another language* (2nd ed.). Cambridge, England: Cambridge University Press.

Norris, J., & Ortega, L. (2000). Effectiveness of L2 instruction: A research synthesis and quantitative meta-analysis. *Language Learning, 50*, 417–528. doi:10.1111/0023-8333.00136

Pfenninger, S. E., & Singleton, D. (2017). *Beyond age effects in instructional L2 learning: Revisiting the age factor*. Bristol, England: Multilingual Matters.

Renandya, W. A. (2013). The role of input- and output-based practice in ELT. In A. Ahmed, M. Hanzala, F. Saleem, & G. Cane (Eds.), *ELT in a changing world* (pp. 41–52). Newcastle-upon-Tyne, England: Cambridge Scholars.

Sato, R. (2009). Considering the effectiveness of recasts on Japanese high school learners' learning. *Journal of Asia TEFL, 6*(4), 193–216.

Scovel, T. (2001). *Learning new languages: A guide to second language acquisition*. Boston, MA: Heinle & Heinle.

Spada, N. (2011). Beyond form-focused instruction: Reflections on past, present and future research. *Language Teaching, 44*, 225–236. doi:10.1017/S0261444810000224

Spada, N. (2015). SLA research and L2 pedagogy: Misapplications and questions of relevance. *Language Teaching, 48*, 69–81. doi:10.1017/S026144481200050X

Spielmann, G., & Radnofsky, M. L. (2001). Learning language under tension: New directions from a qualitative study. *Modern Language Journal, 85*, 259–278. doi:10.1111/0026-7902.00108

Strid, J. E. (2017). The myth of the critical period. *TESOL Journal, 8*, 700–715. doi:10.1002/tesj.296

Swain, M. (1993). The output hypothesis: Just speaking and writing aren't enough. *Canadian Modern Language Review, 50*, 158–164.

Swain, M. (2005). The output hypothesis: Theory and research. In E. Hinkel (Ed.), *Handbook of research in second language teaching and learning* (pp. 471–483). Mahwah, NJ: Lawrence Erlbaum.

Swain, M., Kinnear, P., & Steinman, L. (2015). *Sociocultural theory in second language education: An introduction through narratives* (2nd ed.). Bristol, England: Multilingual Matters.

Tarone, E. (2015). Second language acquisition in applied linguistics: 1925–2015 and beyond. *Applied Linguistics, 36*, 444–453. doi:10.1093/applin/amv035

Tomlinson, B. (2017). Achieving a match between SLA theory and materials development. In B. Tomlinson (Ed.), *Second language acquisition research and materials development for language teaching* (pp. 3–22). London, England: Routledge.

VanPatten, B. (2003). *From input to output: A teacher's guide to second language acquisition*. New York, NY: McGraw-Hill.

VanPatten, B. (2017). Situating instructed language acquisition: Facts about second language acquisition. *Instructed Second Language Acquisition, 1*, 45–60. doi:10.1558/isla.33315